EDUARDO BLACKMORE

The Book of Female Singers Incredible Facts

Discover the Life, Voice and Music of Incredible Female Singers, plus Extra Trivia Quizzes.

This book was professionally typeset on Reedsy.
Find out more at reedsy.com

Contents

Introduction

Do you love Female Singers? What's not to love about them? I've always been so attracted to the nice, warm and beautiful voice of a singer like Aretha Franklin, Adele or Whitney Houston, or maybe you enjoy the strong, powerful and empowering voice of Alicia Keys, Christina Aguilera or Carole King. Their voice has made us dream, fall in love, love them, cry, and embrace the feminine side both men and women have. When we hear them, I think we don't just enjoy music, but we are also experiencing the voice of the most important woman in our lives, our mothers, our sisters, our lovers, and our daughters. This book is a celebration of their greatness, the recognition from my soul of what they mean in my life, and an invitation to discover some singers that we might haven't heard about but could be part of your life from now on.

We love Female Singer's voices because they are soothing and calming, there's something about a woman's voice that just makes us feel at ease, and the female singers we will review have some of the most beautiful voices in the music industry. Technically speaking, female singers often have powerful vocal ranges that allow them to sing a variety of genres, thus, their voices can make us feel happy or sad, depending on the song they are performing.

These artists have all achieved success with their music, either globally or locally, and usually, their music often has a positive message that speaks to their fans. It is not uncommon for them to use their platform to advocate for social causes.

We love hearing stories about women and their personal lives and how they became singers or songwriters, it is always inspirational to us. One story that I particularly love is that of Whitney Houston. She was one of the most successful singers of all time, but her life was not easy. She came from a very poor family and had to drop out of school to help support them. Despite all of this, she never gave up on her dream of becoming a singer. And she eventually made it, becoming one of the most iconic vocalists of our generation. Another incredible story is that of Celine Dion. She was born into a large family in Canada and had to work hard to make ends meet. But she never gave up on her dream of becoming a singer. And she eventually became one of the most successful singers in the world. These are just two of the many stories of people who have overcome adversity to achieve their dreams. And they show that, no matter what life throws at you, if you never give up on your dreams, anything is possible.

If you're a music lover, then you're probably familiar with some of the world's most popular singers. But did you know that there are many other fantastic singers out there who don't always get the same recognition? That's why in this book I won't only talk about globally acclaimed singers, but also fewer known ones, like Spanish and Italian singers, among others.

The First Part of this book is about the Life, Voice, albums, and songs of Female Singers that have been part of my musical journey, and personally like, but who may not necessarily be that familiar to most people. It will be an invitation to discover these and other singers that you may never have heard of. You will find their music on almost all music streaming services.

The Second Part has an extra 12 Trivia Quizzes about Female Singers in general, where we will find facts about the greatest singers of all times, from Aretha Franklin to Lizzo!

Part One

Their Life. Their Voice. Their Music.

KT Tunstall

Her life

It's another episode of Jools Holland's TV show in 2004, an unknown girl with a guitar and some effect pedals exquisitely played as a single woman band a vibrant song called "Black Horse and the Cherry Tree". The beautiful husky voice filled the stage for 3 minutes and 35 seconds. 24 hours before she didn't know she was going to perform that night, she was chosen to fill out for an artist that couldn't make it that day. The rest is history, she became an "instant" success, and even got a Grammy nomination for that song. She is Scottish and her name is KT Tunstall. She was adopted shortly after her birth to a rather unmusical family and somehow, she managed to learn piano, flute, and guitar early in life.

Her voice

She has an unmistakable timbre, a beautifully smoky and soulful voice, mixed with a youthful energy that lifts any moment, creating a cozy and familiar atmosphere whatever the moment you meet her and her music. She is a talented guitarist and often uses percussive elements in her music. Of course, it's pop music, but mixed with some folk and indie, that's why we've all heard some of her songs. Her song "Suddenly

I See" is everything she's said likes about music: inviting, mixed with mystery, and a little fright.She has been compared to artists such as Sheryl Crow, Stevie Nicks, and Melissa Etheridge.

Best Album/Song

Eye to the Telescope. The album was first released in 2004, didn't get very much attention the first time. Then released again in 2005 in the U.K. and in 2006 in the U.S.A., where rose steadily in the rankings and had a presence in movies and in the hearts of all those who love her voice. Later, the album became multi-platinum around the world.

Sole Gimenez

Her life

Soledad Gimenez is her real name, she was born in France, then moved to Spain when she was 5 years old. First, she joined some choirs, and later with her older brother and other friends she created the band **"Presuntos Implicados"**, which initially had 11 members and was later reduced to 3. She was the singer of course.

Her voice

Her peaceful, silvery voice is an absolute gift for those who love female singers, mysterious and vibrant, she is the perfect companion for the jazz-oriented music her band plays. Every note is like they are right beside the listener, and being sung in Spanish, it is a double gift every time.

Best Album/Song

Her best Album is "Ser de Agua". From the song "Como hemos cambiado", which talks about how one changes through every stage of life, and "Llovio" which describes the weakness of love when it is stalked by the rains of life, to "Icaro" which recreates the story of Icarus, a character from Greek mythology, every piece of the puzzle fits perfectly to create a unique experience. A special mention for "Recibes Cartas", which has this wonderful line:

"It seems like I forgot where I'm from,
from saying goodbye so much"

Luz Casal

H**er life**

This Spanish singer was born in Baimorto, La Coruna in 1958. She started as a rock singer, before starting a solo career. She moved to Madrid in 1977 and started to create a name for herself, after years of solid growth came massive success, in 1991 she released "A contraluz", which became four-time platinum.

Her voice

She has a strong, vibrant voice, full of emotion and thickness, reaching one of its peaks in the song "Piensa en Mi", a bolero chosen by film director Pedro Almodóvar for his mythical movies "Tacones Lejanos".

Best Album/Song

"Mi confianza" is a song on the album "Un mar de confianza", that displays all of her voice, in a more mature stage of her life, full of reminiscence and melancholia, although it talks about how she has grown to have complete confidence in life, love, and humanity, the song is summed up in this sentence:

"Two impulses and a single being,
making me believe that I can stay standing"

Sandra Mihanovic

Her life

She is an Argentinian singer and actress, that acquired her love for music from her paternal grandfather since in his house it was usual to find jazz musicians playing every week. At her grandfather's house, she began to sing as a child, then learned to play the guitar with her uncles and aunts.

Her voice

She has explored various genres and can sing either jazz, ballads, rock, or pop. She has an honest, powerful, and tuned throaty voice, and deeply conveys the feelings expressed by lyrics in every song.

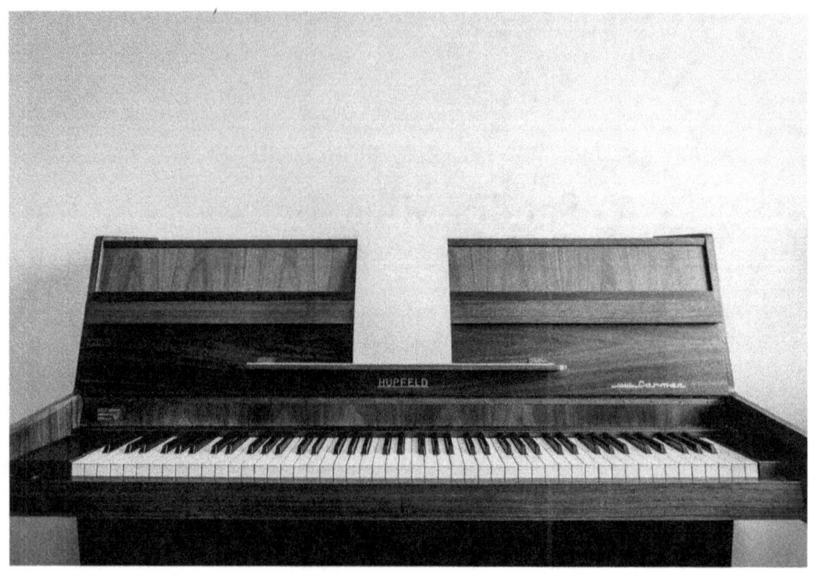

Best Album/Song

Her best song is "Como el Padre Sol". This song is part of the album "Hagamos el Amor", released in 1983, it's the beautiful and heartbreaking cry of someone who loves, who loves so deeply that he compares that love to the sun itself. She is at the same time happy and overwhelmed by this love. The key phrase in which she offers to her love: "my taste and my smell… all my humanity".

Eddie Brickell

Her life

Born in Dallas, Texas, she only started singing when was invited one night to play with a local band, The New Bohemians, that night they would improvise out of nothing, and they were hooked. Three years later they released their debut album "Shooting Rubberbands at the Stars". Sometime later she married the legendary singer, Paul Simon.

Her voice

She is a trademark from the 80's decade, "What I am" was a slap in the face to the reigning materialism from that time. Her voice is soft and personal, she "wanders" when she sings, like she is timidly trying to follow the melody of the song, but without straying from her original intention. She herself is a shy person, that tries to invite whoever listens to her world.

Best Album/Song

Good Times. She released this song without the New Bohemians, this song has an incredible smoothness, it's as if she were singing it in your living room and at the same time in front of the whole world, with that trait of closeness and shyness so typical of Edie Brickell.

Martika

Her life

Her real name is Marta Marrero, born in California to Cuban parents. She started her career with a minor role in the 1982 movie Annie, later landing in the children's TV Show Kids Incorporated in which sounds of her adult voice could already be heard.

Her voice

She can transition from a tremendously warm voice to a stormy one in the same line, precise in each tone, which you can hear in the few live recordings that can be found on the web. She sings in Spanish, but there are not many recordings or videos available of her doing so.

Best Album/Song

Toy Soldiers. It's her greatest hit so far, she also co-wrote the song, and here she delivers what we love the most about her, her vibrato, tenderness of the verses, and a strong chorus, where she displays her full voice range, it's both euphoric and melodic.

Ana Torroja

Her life

Born in Madrid, to parents who had nothing to do with the musical world. She was the voice of one of the greatest bands of Spain: Mecano. The hallmark of Mecano's songs was that Ana always sang from a male perspective since the lyrics were mainly written by the Cano brothers, who completed the trio.

Her voice

She has a silky and soft, yet strong voice, that expresses feelings in each sentence. One of the most particular voices I have ever heard, it's just a gift to anyone who listens to it, and that leaves you wanting to hear many more songs.

Best Album/Song

There are so many songs I could mention, and still I would run short regarding Ana Torroja, three of her best are "Hijo de la Luna", "Me cuesta tanto olvidarte" y "Mujer contra mujer". The best thing you could do to discover her is just look for a full playlist by her and playing it all day long.

Carole King

Her life

One of the greatest singer-songwriters of all time, born Carol Joan Klein started her musical career before she was 15 years old. Her first hit song as co-writer was "Will You Love Me Tomorrow", it became a number one single the year she turned 19. Later on, among other hits, she also co-wrote "The Loco-Motion", "(You Make Me Feel like) A Natural Woman", recorded by the legendary Aretha Franklin, and "You've Got a Friend".

Now, all that happened before 1971, when she launched Tapestry, the album that would really take her to another dimension, musically speaking. From this album, she was awarded four Grammy Awards, Album of the Year, Best song, Best Single, and Best Female Vocal Performance. Tapestry included also "I Feel the Earth Move" and "It's Too Late", among others.

Her voice

Carole King has said that she used to hate her voice, and as we've seen so far, she didn't sing most of her songs at first, and it's fair to say that she doesn't have the greatest voice range of all times, but there's something about that husky, hoarse voice, that pleases everyone who listens to it.

Now, such well-written, relatable songs, makes it much easier to get hooked by her voice. Personally, I prefer most of her songs when they are sung by her than by other artists.

Best Album/Song

Tapestry wasn't her first album as a solo artist, but it really was the most prolific and popular of them all, as we've seen. Many artists have made their own versions of Carole King's songs, such as Martika (I Feel the Earth Move), Gloria Estefan (It's too Late), and Kylie Minogue (Locomotion), just to name a few of them.

Among many awards, she was inducted into the Songwriters Hall of Fame in 1987, received a Grammy Award for lifetime achievement, and was named a Kennedy Center honoree in 2015, and was also inducted into the Rock and Roll Hall of Fame in 2021, you can find who sang her famous song "Will you Love me Tomorrow" that night in the Trivia of this book!

Laura Pausini

Her life

She is the most successful and famous Italian singer of all time, born in the city of Faenza, she started as a piano bar singer, along with her father. She competed in various singing competitions, but her big break came in 1993 when she won the Newcomers' Section of the 43rd Sanremo Music Festival with the song "La Solitudine". Pausini's debut album, "Laura Pausini", was released in Italy in May 1993 and later in the rest of Europe.

Her voice

Pausini is an outstanding singer with great vocal control, her voice is distinctive and unique, yet sweet and fragile sounding. Pausini's vocal range spans over three octaves. She is able to hold long notes without wavering or losing the pitch. Her voice has a lot of emotion and feeling, which is evident in her live performances. Her lyrics are simple and direct, but they are also very poetic.

Best Album/Song

Laura Pausini's best album is the mentioned "Laura Pausini" from 1993, it was a huge success, selling over two million copies worldwide. It spawned the hit singles "La Solitudine", "Strani Amori", and "Gente".

Bebe Rexha

Her life

Bebe Rexha is an American singer, songwriter, and record producer. She is known for songs such as "Meant to Be" with Florida Georgia Line, "In the Name of Love" with Martin Garrix, and "I Got You" which was used as the Coca-Cola Anthem for the 2016 Summer Olympics. Rexha was born and raised in Brooklyn, New York to Albanian parents. She began singing at an early age and started songwriting when she was just 14 years old. Rexha rose to prominence in 2015 with her feature on G-Eazy's single "Me, Myself & I". The song peaked at number seven on the Billboard Hot 100, making it Rexha's first top ten single as a lead artist.

Her voice

Bebe Rexha's voice has been described as "raw" with "edgy raspiness". The Fader has said that her vocal range is "unusual for a pop singer". Rexha also plays guitar and piano. She wrote all 14 songs on her 2014 EP, I Don't Wanna Grow Up. Bebe Rexha's musical influences come from a mix of pop and rock music. She has cited Nicki Minaj, Katy Perry, Rihanna, Bruno Mars, and Linkin Park as her musical influences. Rexha also has a love for country music; she has said that Taylor Swift is one of her favorite songwriters.

Best Album/Song

Bebe Rexha's debut album, "Expectations," is her best album to date. The album was released in 2018 and features the hit single, "Meant to Be." The album is a mix of pop, R&B, and hip-hop, and showcases Rexha's incredible vocal range. "Expectations" is an incredibly personal album, with Rexha opening about her struggles with anxiety and depression. The album is a must-listen for any Bebe Rexha fan and will leave you eager for more.

Camila Cabello

Her life

Camila Cabello is a Cuban American singer and songwriter. Her early life was really challenging, she and her mom crossed the Mexican border when she was 7 years old, leaving her dad in Mexico. She rose to prominence as a member of the girl group Fifth Harmony, formed on The X Factor (U.S.) in 2012, signing a joint record deal with Syco Music and Epic Records. After leaving the group in December 2016, Cabello released several other singles, including "I Have Questions" and "Bad Things". "Havana", featuring Young Thug, peaked at number two on the Hot 100, becoming her highest-charting single as a solo artist. "Havana" also topped charts in Australia, Canada, the United Kingdom, and several other countries.

Her voice

She has one of the most unique and special voices in music today. She has a very wide vocal range and is able to hit some extremely high notes. Her voice is also very powerful and can really fill a room. When you listen to any Firth Harmony song, you can hear Camila everywhere, I think she was the big star of that band and she is the singer of the band that has had the most success in her solo career.

Best Album/Song

Her album Familia is my favorite. I love the mix of genres on it and her voice is so unique. If you haven't listened to it yet, I highly recommend doing so! You won't be disappointed. I love each and every song, but especially "Me duelen hasta los dientes", featuring Argentinian singer Maria Becerra, and "Don't go Yet", a great Latin-influenced pop song, she mentioned that references her relationship with singer Shawn Mendes, and how she wanted to stay at some parties longer than him.

Alessia Cara

Her life

Cara was born and raised in Toronto, Ontario. She is of Italian descent from her paternal grandparents, who immigrated to Canada from Buccino in the province of Salerno, and of Irish descent from her maternal grandparents. As a child, she sang in church choirs and took voice lessons, but left formal training at age 13 to pursue a career in music, she made a deal with her parents, that if there was no evidence of success for one year after leaving formal studies, she would go back to study. During that year she was signed by a music label.

Alessia Cara's life changed the night she won a Grammy for her debut album, Know-It-All. The singer-songwriter from Toronto was working at Starbucks and writing songs in her bedroom just a few years before that. Cara's music career took off when her friend posted a song she had written and recorded on YouTube.

Her voice

Her voice has been described as warm, natural, and emotive, with a clear tone that allows her lyrics to shine through. Her music is often compared to that of Amy Winehouse, Adele, and other soul/R&B singers.

Cara's lyrics have been praised for their relatable and personal nature, with many fans finding comfort and connection in her words.

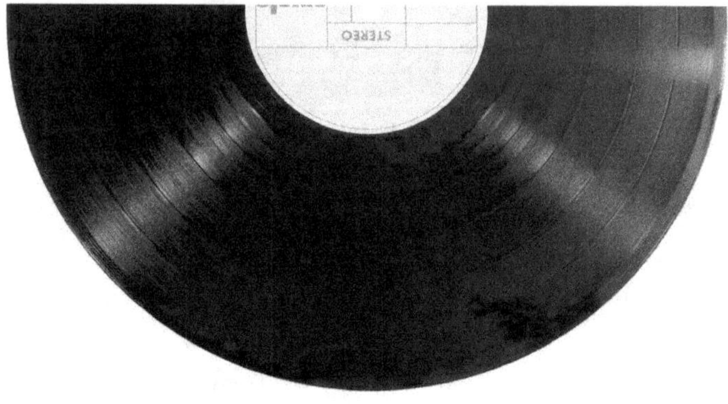

Best Album/Song

For me, her best song is "Scars to Your Beautiful", a pop ballad that talks about body image awareness. She was motivated to write this song after watching a TV Show, you can find what TV Show was in the Trivia of this book!

Part Two

Extra Trivia Quizzes

QUIZ #1

1. What song was written in 1970, released for the first time in 1978, and then became the first #1 Whitney Houston song, eight years later?
2. What singer-songwriter co-wrote "Hey Mama", wasn't initially credited on it, and also co-wrote Eminem's smash hit "The Monster".
3. What Australian singer/songwriter wanted, in her own words, "just to be a writer for other artists".
4. What song by Aretha Franklin is a cover?
5. Celine Dion won the popular Eurovision Song Contest, but she didn't win the prize for Canada, she won it on behalf of what country?

Answers

1. "Saving all my love for you"
2. Bebe Rexha.
3. Sia.
4. "Respect" is a cover of an Otis Redding song. Franklin rewrote the lyrics, and the song became her first number one hit song.
5. Switzerland.

QUIZ #2

1. How much time took Dolly Parton to write the legendary songs "Jolene" and "I Will Always Love You"?
2. Taylor Swift was named after what famous artist?
3. Who was Jessie J.'s classmate at the same performing arts high school and used to sing together at lunch?
4. Sia's "This is Acting" included songs that were originally written for what famous artists?
5. What two artists were partners in a children's T.V. Show?

Answers

1. She wrote both <u>on the same day</u>!
2. Legendary singer-songwriter James Taylor.
3. Adele
4. Rihanna, Beyonce, and Katy Perry.
5. Demi Lovato and Selena Gomez worked together on "Barney & Friends".

QUIZ #3

1. What hit song by Joan Jett is a cover?
2. What Britney Spears song was intended initially for TLC?
3. "I'm A Slave 4 U" was going to be recorded by which renowned singer instead of Britney Spears?
4. Incredibly, the hit song "Torn", which launched the career of Natalie Imbruglia is a cover! How many artists do you think performed the song prior to Imbruglia?
5. What Cindy Lauper song was a cover?

Answers

1. I Love Rock 'N Roll" is a cover by the English band The Arrows.
2. "Baby One More Time".
3. Janet Jackson.
4. It was recorded and released by three artists, American band Ednaswap, singer Lis Sorensen (Danish version), and by American-Norwegian singer Trine Rein. The song was written in 1993 and was only recorded by Imbruglia in 1997.
5. "Girls Just Wanna Have Fun" is a cover of a song by American musician Robert Hazard. Lauper's version peaked at number 2 on Billboard Hot 100 chart.

QUIZ #4

1. Artist Leona Lewis was originally supposed to sing which Rihanna's hit song?
2. Which hit song was intended for Kylie Minogue instead of Britney Spears.
3. What Kelly Clarkson hit was first turned down by Pink and Hilary Duff?
4. Kylie Minogue sang a famous hit that was written for Britain band S Club 7. Can you name it?
5. "Hero" by Mariah Carey was originally intended for which singer originally?

Answers

1. We Found Love".
2. "Toxic"
3. "Since U Been Gone"
4. "Can't Get You Out of My Head"
5. Gloria Estefan.

QUIZ #5

1. Which of Whitney Houston's former hits re-entered the Billboard Hot 100 chart after her death in 2012?
2. How many American Music Awards did Houston win?
3. How many consecutive No. 1 singles did Houston have on the U.S. Billboard Hot 100?
4. What role did Ariana play in the Nickelodeon television series Victorious?
5. Where did Lady Gaga get that famous name from?

Answers

1. "I Will Always Love You", "I Wanna Dance with Somebody (Who Loves Me), and "Greatest Love of All".
2. 22 American Music Awards.
3. Seven consecutive number-one singles on the U.S. Billboard Hot 100 chart.
4. Caterina "Cat" Valentine, she was one of Tori's strangest friends from Hollywood Arts High School.
5. From the Queen song "Radio Ga Ga".

QUIZ #6

1. In 2009, Guinness World Records cited her as the most awarded female act of all time.
2. This jazz vocalist, known for her phenomenal vocal range, won 13 Grammys.
3. What famous female pop singer has also won an Academy Award for best actress.
4. Her first five singles topped the U.S. Billboard Hot 100 chart, achieved by no other artist at the time she did it.
5. What was the name of the first all-female rock band to achieve mainstream success?

Answers

1. Whitney Houston.
2. Ella Fitzgerald
3. Cher.
4. Mariah Carey.
5. The Ronettes, an American group from the 1960s.

QUIZ #7

1. Who was the lead singer of The Supremes?
2. Which female vocalist has won the most Grammy Awards?
3. What is the best-selling album by a female vocalist?
4. What is the best-selling album by a female group of all time?
5. Who is the only female artist to have won the Grammy Award for Album of the Year twice?

Answers

1. Diana Ross.
2. Alison Krauss, a bluegrass-country singer and musician. She has won 27 Grammy Awards, the most of any female artist in history.
3. Whitney Houston's The Bodyguard soundtrack, it has sold more than 45 million copies worldwide.
4. The Supremes' Greatest Hits Album has sold more than 22 million copies worldwide.
5. Taylor Swift won the award in 2010 for Fearless and again in 2016 for 1989.

QUIZ #8

1. Which female artist has the most number-one singles on the Billboard Hot 100 chart?
2. What singer-songwriter was best known for her 1997 anthem, "Bitch"?
3. In 1990, Sinead O'Connor scored a number one hit with "Nothing Compares 2U", written by which legendary artist?
4. LeAnn Rimes topped the charts in 1996 with her single, "Blue." How old was Rimes when the single debuted?
5. What female singer, songwriter, and actress appeared in the TV series "As The World Turns".

Answers

1. Mariah Carey, with 18 number-one singles.
2. Meredith Brooks.
3. Prince.
4. 13 years old.
5. Lauryn Hill.

QUIZ #9

1. What singer managed to win a Grammy Award for a song she wrote when she was just 17 years old?
2. Which Canadian-born artist started her career with the album "Jagged Little Pill"?
3. Which rocker became the first woman to perform glam rock?
4. Which artist known for her hoarse voice wrote the hit song "I Can't Make You Love Me"?
5. What singer holds the record of having a Billboard number one hit in each of the last four decades?

Answers

1. Fiona Apple.
2. Alanis Morrisette.
3. Lita Ford.
4. Bonnie Raitt.
5. Mariah Carey

QUIZ #10

1. Name the winner of the first American Idol?
2. Which singer-songwriter has written songs for Britney Spears, Miley Cyrus, and Ariana Grande, among others?
3. Hit song "Wrecking Ball," was offered to which singer before being recorded by Miley Cyrus?
4. Which Grammy Award Winner's real name is Melissa Viviane Jefferson? (By the way, she also performs the hit song "About Damn Time").
5. What instrument does the famous singer Lizzo play perfectly?

Answers

1. Kelly Clarkson.
2. Kesha.
3. Beyoncé.
4. Lizzo.
5. Flute.

QUIZ #11

1. What song from 1985 resurged in 2022 thanks to the "Stranger Things" series, and who sings it?
2. Which English singer bet heavily on releasing her album during the Covid 19 pandemic, and now is considered one of the best albums of the 21st century?
3. Which famous singer performed Carole King's hit "Will you Love me Tomorrow" the night King was inducted into the Rock and Roll Hall of Fame in the year 2021?
4. What TV Show motivated Alessia Cara to write the song "Scars to Your Beautiful"?
5. She is part of the "nobility" of music, her cousin is Dionne Warwick, and her godmother is Aretha Franklin.

Answers

1. The song is "Running Up That Hill", by English singer and songwriter Kate Bush from her album, Hounds of Love.
2. Dua Lipa.
3. Taylor Swift.
4. Botched.
5. Whitney Houston.

Conclusion

There is something special about a woman's voice that touches our hearts. Perhaps it is the range of emotions they can convey in their songs, or the fact that they often write their own material. We love to hear their stories of how they became singers, and what drives them to share their music with the world. Female singers have a unique ability to connect with us on an emotional level, and we appreciate their talent for delivering beautiful vocal performances.

The female singers of today have truly shown us that women can do anything they set their minds to. They have fought for their place in the music industry and have carved out a path for future generations of female artists. These women are strong, powerful, and talented; they are true role models for young girls everywhere. I hope you have enjoyed learning about these amazing women and their contributions to the music industry. Thank you for reading!

If you found this book helpful, I'd be very appreciative if you left a favorable review for the book on Amazon!

Resources

- 32 Random Music Facts You Probably Didn't Know Until Reading This Post. **https://www.google.com/amp/s/www.buzzfeed.com/amphtml/kaylayandoli/random-music-facts**
- Whitney Houston. **https://en.wikipedia.org/wiki/Whitney_Houston**
- 16 Surprising Facts You Didn't Know About Popular Songs. **https://www.google.com/amp/s/www.businessinsider.com/surprising-facts-about-popular-songs-2014-4%3famp**
- 65 Random Song Facts That Will Change Your Life. **https://wjbq.com/65-random-song-facts-that-will-change-your-life/**
- 65 Songs You Will Never Be Able To Listen To The Same Way Again. **https://www.buzzfeed.com/mjs538/songs-youll-never-be-able-to-listen-to-the-same-way-again?bffb**
- Soledad Giménez. **https://simple.wikipedia.org/wiki/Soledad_Gim%C3%A9nez**
- KT Tunstall Biography and Life Story. **https://www.aceshowbiz.com/celebrity/kt_tunstall/biography.html**
- Luz Casal. **https://en.wikipedia.org/wiki/Luz_Casal**
- Sandra Mihanovic. https://es.wikipedia.org/wiki/Sandra_Mihanovich
- Edie Brickell. https://en.wikipedia.org/wiki/Edie_Brickell

- Martika. https://en.wikipedia.org/wiki/Martika
- Carole King. https://en.wikipedia.org/wiki/Carole_King